# THE STORY OF
# SACAJAWEA,
## Guide to Lewis and Clark

BY DELLA ROWLAND

ILLUSTRATED BY RICHARD LEONARD

A YEARLING BOOK

## ABOUT THIS BOOK

The events described in this book are true. The dialogue has been carefully researched and excerpted from authentic biographies, writings, and commentaries. No part of this biography has been fictionalized.

To learn more about Sacajawea and the Lewis and Clark expedition, ask your librarian to recommend other fine books you might read.

*To Dad*

Published by
Dell Publishing
a division of
Bantam Doubleday Dell Publishing Group, Inc.
666 Fifth Avenue
New York, New York 10103

ISBN: 0-440-40215-8

Published by arrangement with Parachute Press, Inc.

Printed in the United States of America
September 1989

10  9  8  7  6  5  4  3  2  1

CWO

# Contents

# A NEW LIFE

Long ago, safely nestled in a valley of the Bitterroot Mountains, in what we now know as the state of Idaho, was a large village of Shoshoni Indians. In this village lived a young girl who would become famous around the world. Today, we know her as Sacajawea—a name that came from a tribe different from her own. Then, when she was still a young girl, she might have been known as Huichu, meaning Little Bird. This was a common name given to Shoshoni girls. According to Shoshoni tradition, she would have had several different names throughout her childhood.

In 1800, Little Bird was celebrating her twelfth summer. Although she didn't know it, her way of life would soon change. The white Americans who lived far to the east were soon to come west. Her life and theirs would become closely bound and, together, they would make an important contribution to American history.

Little Bird was the daughter of an important Shoshoni leader. The Shoshoni were a nomadic tribe; they moved with the change in seasons in order to gather the food they needed to eat. Each spring they traveled west to the Camas Prairie to dig up the delicious roots of the bright blue camas lily. During the summer they returned to the

1

mountain rivers to fish for the salmon that were swimming upstream to lay their eggs. And every fall they crossed the mountains to the eastern plains to hunt among the vast herds of buffalo there.

Long ago, they had learned the seasons of plants and animals and the right time to pick or hunt them. In the rocky forests they could snare rabbits, foxes, and wolves and find the shy deer and elk. They had even learned how to catch the bighorn sheep that leaped along the steep mountainsides. The Shoshoni women knew where to find more than one hundred different plants. Little Bird's people were proud that they knew how to live from the gifts of nature. But the Shoshoni hadn't always lived in this way.

The elders told stories around the evening campfires of a different way of life, before their people had horses. That was thousands of years ago, when the Shoshoni Indians had lived in the rough country west of what we now know as the Rocky Mountains. There had been many tribes then, and although their vast land had many lush green valleys full of game, the tribes still needed to roam the mountains and plains to search for food.

With horses they got from Spanish settlements in New Mexico, the Shoshoni began traveling longer distances. Shoshoni nomads could soon be found over thousands of miles, moving from place to place wherever food was available. But smallpox epidemics made them weak, allowing their enemies to take advantage of them. Some of the tribes went into the mountains for safety.

Riding east of the glistening Rocky Mountains across the Great Plains, they depended upon the buffalo for food and other necessities. They liked the taste of the buffalo's meat, and they used the hide to make the warm robes that they needed to survive the winters. Long before 1800, they had become skilled hunters, training their horses to cut and turn through the herds, even without a rider on them.

Some Plains Indians felt threatened by the Shoshoni. They wanted to drive the Shoshoni back into the mountains, but the Shoshoni were more powerful because they had horses. Then, other Plains Indians began getting guns from the French fur traders who came down from Canada. Gradually, they obtained horses, too, and began to win battles against camp after camp of Shoshoni. Finally the Shoshoni were forced back into the mountains.

Now Little Bird's people came down from the mountains to hunt with great caution. When they were on the plains, they worked quickly. As soon as the men killed the buffalo, the women dried the meat and tanned the skins. When they had all they could carry, they hurried back into the mountains.

Little Bird's father always knew when it was time to leave the mountains to hunt for buffalo. This year, as always, his people had dried camas roots and salmon to eat in the cold months ahead. But this food wouldn't last all winter, and the Shoshoni needed warm hides for winter robes. He decided. It was time to move to the buffalo hunting grounds.

Little Bird's village was bustling as they prepared for their journey. Even though she was still a child, Little Bird did some of the work of a woman. That morning she helped her mother take down the tepee and bundle up the family's cooking baskets and sleeping robes. Little Bird and her mother laid their belongings on carriers made out of long poles, then tied the carriers to their horses.

Soon they were off, some riding and some walking beside the animals. At what is now known as the Lehmi Pass they crossed through the mountains and sighted their guide mark, the towering Beaver's Head Rock. In just a few days they reached "the place where three rivers flow into one."

The Indians were excited, but they were nervous, too. They knew that there was always the danger of being attacked by the Minnetaree and Blackfeet Indians, their enemies who lived on the plains. Although the Shoshoni were fierce warriors—they had bows, arrows, and strong shields—their weapons were no match for the guns of the Plains Indians. These tribes made raids on the Shoshoni whenever they found them, carrying off horses and prisoners. Little Bird's people had to be careful at all times.

The three rivers on the plains came from cold underground springs. They were so clear that Little Bird could see the pebbles at the bottom when she knelt down to drink the bright water. She had to walk carefully among the prickly pear and rose briars that grew along the banks.

The rivers were dotted with beaver dams and sandbars. Little Bird could hear the loud sound the beavers made as they slapped their tails on the water. She watched the ducks floating on the rivers and pecking at the thick prairie grass. Beyond the prairie she could see the snow-covered tops of the Rocky Mountains. The glistening caps of snow that covered their peaks made these mountains look as if they were shining.

Returning from the riverbank, Little Bird hurried back to camp to help her mother put up the tepee and build a cooking fire. Some of the men had already ridden off to scout for buffalo. The men in the tribe had three jobs. Their main duty, when they were old enough, was to fight off their enemies. Their second job was to hunt and fish. They also took care of the best horses which were used only for fighting and hunting. Little Bird's brothers were old enough now to go on the hunt.

"Buffalo! Buffalo!" The women looked up from the fire as the scouts galloped through the camp crying out that they had found a herd. The men sat down to discuss a plan for the hunt. That night everyone ate dried salmon and thought about the buffalo meat they would have the next day!

Early the next morning the men and older boys rode out to the herd. They killed as many buffalo as they could, leaving the animals where they dropped. The women followed them. As soon as it was safe, they rode out to the dead buffalo and began skinning them.

Cutting through the thick hide of a buffalo was hard work. After the women pulled back the skin, they hacked off small pieces of meat. Immediately everyone on the hunt ate as much raw meat as they could. They did so because there was always the danger that an enemy could swoop down on them suddenly and take their kill. Even if they lost what was left, at least they would have had something to fill their stomachs that day.

The rest of the buffalo meat was piled on the carriers to take back to camp. There the elders and children who stayed behind would feast on it. What was left would be dried and saved for future needs.

As soon as the women got back to camp, the hides had to be tanned for making robes and moccasins. During the day, the robes were worn as coats and at night they were used as blankets. To provide extra warmth for the winter that was coming, the thick wool was left on the hide.

After the tanning was finished, Little Bird and her friends went out to the plains to gather plants and berries. They picked choke cherries and purple, black, red, and yellow currants. The mountain currants that grew on the cliffs weren't very tasty, so the girls left them alone. Little Bird knew most of the plants her people used for food or medicine. Her mother had taught her where they grew and how to tell when they were ready to be picked.

When they weren't out hunting, Little Bird's brothers played hunting games—shooting arrows

6

or racing horses. There were always foot races or wrestling matches going on among the boys. They also played a game in which the players tried to kick each other's legs. Sometimes a boy got knocked down, but no one was ever seriously hurt. It was all fun and good training for hunting and fighting.

The girls and women didn't have as much time for games. They were too busy with the daily chores. But when Little Bird wasn't helping her mother, she, too, loved to play with her friends. The girls liked to play cat's cradle, using string made of braided sagebrush grass to thread through their fingers. Sometimes they would play with dolls made from willows or woven wicker.

In the evening, everyone gathered together to watch folk tales being performed by the skilled elder tellers. One storyteller would play the many different parts of traditional birds and animals. To tell the story, he would speak in a different musical tone for each part he played. For instance, he would speak in one tone for Owl, in another for Coyote, and in yet another for Bear. These stories told all about Shoshoni tradition and culture.

One day, not long after they had arrived at their winter hunting grounds, Little Bird's people were surprised by a group of Minnetarees, an enemy tribe from the east who had discovered their camp. All at once the air was filled with shouting and gunshots.

Many of the men were out scouting that day. Those who were left at camp were defenseless and outnumbered. Some hopped on their horses, as the

7

women grabbed up the small children. Those on foot ran along the widest of the three rivers to a woods three miles away and huddled in the trees and bushes. The women pinched the noses of their babies to keep them from making a sound.

Suddenly the enemy's horses thundered through the woods. Little Bird began to run again. But which way should she go? Looking behind her, she saw the Minnetarees shooting the men who were trying to escape. Then, to her horror, she saw that they were killing the women and children, too!

Gunshots and the cries of her friends followed her as she started back toward the river, running as hard as she could. She found a place shallow enough to cross. The river was so cold and swift, she could hardly make her legs move! She was struggling hard to reach the other side when she was suddenly captured by a tall, pale Minnetaree warrior.

The Minnetarees easily rounded up all the women and girls who were left alive. They would all be taken away and used as slaves for the Minnetaree women. Terrified, Little Bird looked frantically for her mother and sister. They were nowhere to be found among the prisoners. Had they escaped? Were her father and brothers safe? Would Little Bird see any of them again?

Suddenly, she saw her best friend. She ran to her and they huddled together. At least they would have each other, whatever happened to them now!

The Minnetarees lined up their captives and headed east across the Great Plains. Little Bird was

pulled along as she turned to look back at the shining mountains. Day after day, she and the other women and children walked. Each mile took her farther from the life she had known and the people she loved. If her family were alive, perhaps they would come for her. But as each sad day passed, her hope of being rescued grew fainter.

Many weeks later, after a journey of five hundred miles, they arrived at the Minnetaree village. It was built on the spot where the Knife and the Missouri rivers meet, near what is now Bismarck, North Dakota. As soon as she entered the village, Little Bird became a slave who belonged to anyone who laid claim to her. Slaves were expected to work hard every day and were sometimes beaten.

Everything around her was confusing and frightening. Her captors told her what to do in a language she didn't understand. Their food and customs were strange. They even looked different. Her people were short and dark, whereas the Minnetarees were tall and light skinned.

The Minnetaree village was very different from Little Bird's. Instead of leather or willow tepees, these people lived in round lodges made of earth and grass. The lodges looked like upside-down bowls. At the top of each one was a hole to let out the campfire smoke.

Little Bird was surprised when she entered one of the earthen lodges and had to step down. The floor had been dug a foot lower than the ground outside. It was smooth and as hard as stone. She looked around. A large fire burned in a pit in the center of the huge room. Buckskin hide curtains had been hung to make separate sleeping quarters. These lodges were much bigger than her people's. Several families lived in each one, along with their supplies of food, and even some horses!

Little Bird quickly realized that the Minnetarees lived in their village all year long. They certainly couldn't move these lodges to another hunting ground the way her people moved their tepees. But how did they find food if they never moved? Little Bird soon found the answer to that question when she went to work.

One of Little Bird's jobs was to help the Minnetaree women tend their fields. The Minnetarees had learned to grow crops from the Mandan Indians, their neighbors across the Missouri River. They raised sunflowers, pumpkins, and tobacco. They had five kinds of beans, nine kinds of corn, and several different types of squash. Little Bird had never seen these vegetables before. She had never planted anything, either. She had only gathered plants that grew wild.

As wanderers, Little Bird's people believed nature gave them their life through the food they gathered, and they looked down on the tribes who planted crops and stayed in one place. But Little Bird could see that the Minnetaree women were expert farmers and that they were proud of their gardens. They were careful to plant each vegetable at a certain time so that it would grow properly.

When spring arrived, Little Bird had to be out in the fields before sunrise. She learned how to use

11

a pointed digging stick to make planting holes. Later she was given a hoe made out of the shoulder blade bone of a buffalo and taught how to weed the rows of growing crops. Her rake was made out of deer antlers tied to a stick.

In the middle of each garden, the women built a platform under a shady tree. There they sat after the crops had been planted to make sure the deer or birds didn't eat the vegetables. While they sat, they sewed and sang to the garden to make it grow. To them the garden was like a baby. They sang to it so that it would be contented and flourish.

Some of the vegetables were eaten fresh out of the garden, but most of them were dried. Little Bird was taught how to cut squash into slices, poke holes in the middle of them, and hang them on poles to dry. She shelled the dried corn and ground it into corn meal or boiled it in lye to make hominy. The Minnetarees stored their dried vegetables in underground cellars. That way, they had enough food to last through the winter.

Besides having enough to eat, life with the Minnetarees was more secure than the existence she had known before. For one thing, the Minnetarees were safer from their enemies. They had guns and a village that was like a fortress. It was built on a bend in the river with a high fence around it. No enemy could get inside. What a difference from Little Bird's people, who could only run from their enemies or stay hidden in the mountains.

Her people also had no protection from the weather. Whenever it snowed, they were cold;

whenever it rained, they were wet. But in the Minnetaree village thick earthen walls kept the lodges warm in the winter and cool in the summer. The sunken floors were dry even when it rained.

While she lived with the Minnetarees, she learned a new way of life and was given a new name Sakaaka Wiiya, meaning Bird Woman. In English, her name came to be spelled as Sacajawea. This new name was not related to her name as a young girl. These Indians didn't speak her language and would not have known what her Shoshoni name was.

For more than three years, she worked hard for her captors. She and her best friend comforted each other when they were frightened or lonely. One day, Sacajawea couldn't find her friend. She had escaped! After she was gone, Sacajawea was lonelier than ever. Should she try to escape, too? Could she find the way home? Or was she too different now to go back to her old life?

Then, one day, Sacajawea discovered that she had been sold to a white fur trader who wanted her for his wife. He was three times older than she was. What would happen to her now? First the Minnetarees had taken her far from her family and the familiar shining mountains. Now they had sold her to a man she didn't even know.

# THE CORPS OF DISCOVERY

Sacajawea didn't have to travel far to her new home. Her husband, Toussaint Charbonneau, had already been living among the Minnetaree and Mandan Indians for several years, working as an interpreter and a fur trapper. Born in Canada, Charbonneau may even have been the first white man to live with these Indians.

Sacajawea soon learned that her husband was a loud, rough man. They spoke to each other in Minnetaree and with sign language. Unfortunately, even though he was an interpreter, Charbonneau didn't speak Minnetaree very well, and Sacajawea often misunderstood her husband. He became impatient and yelled at her when she did something he didn't like. He even hit her sometimes when he was angry.

The Indians didn't have a lot of respect for the short, dark Frenchman. They made fun of his constant bragging. Nevertheless, they were friendly with him.

Charbonneau had taken up the Indian practice of having more than one wife. He was already married to Otter Woman, another Shoshoni Indian slave he had bought. She had a two-year-old son who was named Toussaint, after his father. Soon Sacajawea was expecting a child.

In October, 1804, word came to the Indian villages that a large party of white men was camped nearby. They had traveled up the Missouri River from St. Louis in three big boats. The curious Indians crowded around the riverbank to see them.

The white men called their largest boat a keelboat. It was fifty-five feet long and needed twenty-two men to row it! The Indians were impressed by the huge cannon on its deck. The other boats were long dugouts called pirogues. One was painted white, one red.

Charbonneau heard that the Minnetaree and Mandan chiefs were having council with the two captains of this party. He found out that the party was called the Corps of Discovery. Its captains, Meriwether Lewis and William Clark, were working for President Thomas Jefferson. They had been sent to explore a huge piece of land the United States had just bought from France through an agreement called the Louisiana Purchase.

Up until then, the western border of the United States only went as far as the Mississippi River. At that time there were seventeen states and three territories. The states were Massachusetts, New Hampshire, Vermont, Connecticut, Rhode Island, New York, New Jersey, Pennsylvania, Delaware, Maryland, Virginia, North and South Carolina, Georgia, Ohio, Kentucky, and Tennessee. The three territories were Indiana, South Ohio, and Mississippi.

This new land, called the Louisiana Territory, stretched from the Mississippi to the Rocky Mountains. It included what are now the states of Iowa, Missouri, Arkansas, Oklahoma, Kansas, Nebraska, North and South Dakota, and parts of Montana, Wyoming, Minnesota, Colorado, Texas, and Louisiana.

France had given Spain the Louisiana Territory in 1762, at the end of the Seven Years' War. In October, 1800, France's leader, Napoleon, forced Spain to give back the Louisiana Territory. This move put the United States in a dangerous situation. Spain was a weak country so when it owned the Louisiana Territory no threat was posed to the United States. But France was strong, and Napoleon was determined to conquer the whole world. He wanted to attack the United States both in front, from the Atlantic Ocean, and in back, from the Louisiana Territory. At this time the United States was only twenty-four years old—not yet strong enough to fight the mighty armies of France. Luckily, Napoleon's battle plans failed, and he sold the Louisiana Territory to the United States.

When President Jefferson bought this new territory, he doubled the size of the United States! Increasing the size of the country made it possible for the United States to become one of the most powerful forces in the world. It also gave the country control of the Mississippi River. This was important because now the farmers and trappers in the middle states could ship their goods freely.

But Jefferson had another reason for wanting to buy this land. The United States had a rich fur trade business with China. It was in competition with Britain for this fur trade. All ships from the United States that were going to China had to go around the tip of South America. One trip usually took three years. President Jefferson was hoping there was a way to go by river straight across this new territory. Then the United States would have a quick, safe way to get its furs across the country, to the Pacific Ocean, where they could be shipped to China. If he could discover this waterway, perhaps the United States could even put its main competitor, Great Britain, out of business.

Lewis and Clark's main job was to find that waterway. They planned to travel up the entire Missouri River. From the Indian villages, the river flowed north through what is now North and South Dakota. Then it turned west and went through what would one day be Montana, to the Rocky Mountains. The captains hoped to find a river through the mountains that would lead into the Columbia River, which they knew emptied into the Pacific Ocean.

President Jefferson also instructed Lewis and Clark to meet with Indians along the way, to inform them that the territory now belonged to the United States, not France. Jefferson hoped to convince the Indians to supply furs only to the United States. He also wanted them to stop warring with one another so that the fur business would go smoothly and so that settlers could move in. If the Indians were loyal and peaceful, the United States would protect them against their enemies.

Lewis and Clark were to keep journals of their

trip for President Jefferson. He wanted them to describe the rivers and the lands they traveled through, as well as the Indians they met and how the different tribes lived. Jefferson even wanted to know about the trees and flowers and birds and all the new animals they saw.

On November 3, 1804, the Corps began building a fort right across the river from the Minnetaree and Mandan villages. They called it Fort Mandan. Since the river would be frozen during the winter, they'd have to live here until spring. Meanwhile, the captains could gather information about this unexplored territory from the fur trappers and Indians who had been there.

The Minnetaree had made many raids across the new territory, all the way to the Rocky Mountains, so the captains were very eager to talk with them. When Charbonneau told Lewis and Clark that he could speak Minnetaree, they hired him as an interpreter.

In less than three weeks, Fort Mandan was finished. It was V-shaped, with eight small, square houses and two storage rooms. On November 20, the crew moved into their new home. Since Charbonneau was working for the Corps, he and his whole family moved in, too. He was hoping the captains would take him on the expedition as an interpreter.

On Christmas Day, the Corps fired off the cannon on the keelboat in celebration. They danced and ate until nine o'clock that night. The Indians were told that Christmas was an important ceremo-

nial day—a "great medicine day"—for the white men. As she waited for her baby to be born, Sacajawea watched this special ceremony. She noticed that the men exchanged presents. But why did they dance? Her people danced before they went on a hunt, or off to fight. Dancing made them strong and fierce. But dancing made the white men laugh!

During the cold winter days at Fort Mandan, the men sat around the fire. The Minnetarees told the captains what they knew of the new territory and its rivers. The Indians described the Great Falls of the Missouri and the River That Scolds at All Others, now called Maria's River. They said that the Missouri would fork into three small rivers on a plain far to the west. This plain was the fall hunting grounds of the Shoshoni. Beyond the Three Forks were the ranges of what Sacajawea described as the shining mountains.

The Indians said there was no river through these tall, rugged mountains; the white men would have to cross them on horse. And they could only get horses from the Shoshoni Indians who lived there. That would be difficult, because the Shoshoni stayed deep in the mountains.

It was clear to the captains that they'd need an interpreter to speak with the Shoshoni. They knew Charbonneau's wife was a Shoshoni, but she was only about sixteen then—and would soon be having a baby. How could they take a young woman with an infant in her arms through this wild, unknown country? It was so important to have an interpreter, however, that the captains decided to talk to her. They'd be able to tell if she was strong enough.

Charbonneau translated between Sacajawea and the captains. They explained that it would be a long, difficult journey, and that they didn't know what to expect. But Sacajawea had become used to traveling when she was a child moving about with her people. She was accustomed to not knowing what to expect from day to day. When she had been kidnapped as a child, she had been forced to learn the Minnetaree way of life. When she became Charbonneau's wife, she had learned to live with his customs. Now she was finding out about the ways of the white people. Sacajawea knew how to adapt to new conditions, and that made her strong and independent.

The captains were convinced she could make it, even carrying her baby. It was settled: Sacajawea was too important to leave behind. She would join the expedition and Charbonneau would, too. Since she didn't speak English, Sacajawea would tell Charbonneau what the Shoshoni said in Minnetaree, and he would translate her words into French. Drewyer, one of the crew members, translated from French into English for the captains.

On the morning of February 11, 1805, Sacajawea felt the first pains of birth. They got worse and worse as the day went on. Finally, around five o'clock, one of the men gave her something to help her. He crumbled up two rings of a rattlesnake's rattle into some water. Ten minutes after she drank it, Sacajawea's son was born! He was named Jean

Baptiste, but everyone called him "Pomp" or "Pompey," which meant "Little Chief."

While the Corps waited for spring to come and the ice to melt on the river, Sacajawea nursed her infant son. As the days got warmer she tried to learn more about the other crew members she would soon be traveling with. The two leaders of the expedition were very different kinds of men. But they had great respect for each other and worked well together.

Handsome, thirty-year-old Meriwether Lewis had been President Jefferson's personal secretary. Earlier, he had been a captain in the United States First Infantry, where he became an experienced military commander. He was also well educated and an excellent scientist who was trained to travel by charting the stars. Lewis was a natural leader, but sometimes he became moody and would burst into anger or become depressed and worried. He could be snobbish, too, and often he liked to be alone.

Lewis had once served under Captain William Clark in the army, and the two had formed a strong friendship then. When Jefferson told Lewis to choose his crew, he immediately asked Clark to be his co-captain, and Clark was quick to say yes.

Thirty-four-year-old William Clark was the youngest brother of George Rogers Clark, a hero of the American Revolution. He was not as well educated as Lewis, but he was an outstanding engineer and map maker, and he was more experienced with boats and water travel than Lewis.

Both captains were exceptional geographers and knew something about medicine, as well.

Clark was a hearty frontiersman. His crew was very fond of him because he was not only a good leader, but also warm and outgoing. The Indians grew to like him, too, and always came to him first with news or problems. They called him the Red-Headed Chief because of his bright red hair.

The captains took thirty-one crew members, most of whom knew how to live in the wilderness. Some of them had special jobs. One was a carpenter, another was a gun maker. There were several good hunters, a blacksmith, and someone who knew how to take care of horses. They had hired the best boatman around, Peter Cruzatte, who was blind in one eye and nearsighted in the other. Cruzatte also had the important job of playing the fiddle. In fact, the list of supplies included a fiddle, a tambourine, and a horn.

Besides Sacajawea and Charbonneau, one other interpreter had been hired, George Drewyer. In addition to being good with languages Drewyer was also an excellent hunter. He knew sign language well. Like Pompey, his father was a French fur trader and his mother, an Indian.

Captain Clark also brought along his servant, York, a black man. The Indians had never seen anyone with black skin before. They called him the Black White Man. Every time he appeared, they gathered around to inspect his hair and dark skin. One Indian even wet his finger and tried to rub off York's skin color! York liked all this attention and usually made himself seem more fierce than he actually was.

There was one more important member of the crew. His name was Scannon, and he was Captain Lewis's big, black Newfoundland dog. Scannon's job was to be a good watchdog and hunter. Later on, he would prove what a valuable member of the crew he was.

Everyone on the trip was expected to pitch in and do whatever had to be done. But one day Charbonneau decided that this arrangement didn't suit him. After all, he was an interpreter. This was a special job and he deserved special treatment. He told the captains he didn't intend to do any work besides interpreting. He informed them that he would leave the expedition whenever he chose to, especially if anyone "miffed" him. And he had to have all the food and supplies he wanted!

These demands were outrageous! The captains couldn't allow any crew member those kinds of privileges. But they also realized that if Charbonneau didn't go on the expedition, neither would Sacajawea, and they needed her. So they decided not to show their anger. Instead, they acted as if they didn't care if Charbonneau left.

Charbonneau was shocked! He didn't expect them to let him go so easily. Now what would he do? In a huff, he moved his family across the river. Suddenly, it did look as if Sacajawea would not go on the expedition—thanks to her husband's vanity.

Fortunately, a few days later, the boastful

Frenchman realized how foolish he had been. He told the captains he was sorry for his hasty actions and agreed to work just like everyone else. The captains breathed a sigh of relief that Sacajawea was still part of the Corps.

As the weather became warmer, it was time for the crew to get the keelboat and pirogues, the canoe-like boats, ready. The ice in the Missouri slowly began breaking up, but the boats were still frozen solid in the river. It took the men four days to hack them free and drag them onto the shore.

The captains, afraid the keelboat might be too big for the rivers ahead, had the men build six canoes to carry the crew and supplies, instead. Then they put sails on the pirogues.

Everything the Corps needed was placed in the boats. Captain Lewis wrote in his journal, "these little vessels contained every article by which we were to expect to subsist or defend ourselves." Tools for blacksmithing and repairing guns were packed, as well as Captain Lewis's instruments to chart the stars. Herbs and medicines were taken to treat illness, and needles and thread to make clothes.

Kegs of pork, flour, parched meal, corn, and dried squash were loaded on, too. For the rest of their food, the crew would have to hunt along the way. An important provision was salt, since it was used to preserve meat; they took seven barrels. They also brought along goods to trade with the

Indians—beads, clothing, pipes, tomahawks, American flags, and medals with President Jefferson's face on them.

Guns were extremely important to the expedition. They were needed for hunting and for protection. Without them, the crew would starve in the wilds or be killed by unfriendly Indians or animals. Since their guns wouldn't fire if their gunpowder was wet, the crew took special precautions to keep the gunpowder dry. It was packed into cannisters made of lead, which were sealed with cork and wax to keep out the water.

There was very little space on the boats, and the Corps had to plan what they took carefully. Still, the men managed to squeeze in some tobacco and "spirits." They even took two lap desks for the captains to write on. In her own slim buckskin bag, called a *parfleche,* Sacajawea packed some pieces of dried bread and sugar to give Pompey later. She had already made a cradleboard in which to carry him on her back.

This small band of people was about to cross several hundred miles of unknown land. They were going to be passing through country for which there were no maps. No one knew what to expect or what dangers they would meet, but everyone was excited and ready to go! Although Sacajawea was not accustomed to showing her emotions openly, before long the crew would find out how much this trip meant to her.

# ON THE MISSOURI RIVER

On April 7, 1805, at four o'clock in the afternoon, the Lewis and Clark expedition left Fort Mandan. That day Captain Lewis wrote in his journal that he was as proud of his "little fleet" as Christopher Columbus or Captain Cook must have been. The crew was jubilant, shouting and waving at the Indians who had come to send them off!

The captains sent the keelboat back to St. Louis with their reports about their winter in Fort Mandan for President Jefferson. They also sent the president more than one hundred local plants, plus trunks containing animal skins and skeletons. There were even three cages of live animals Jefferson had never seen before—a prairie dog, three magpies, and a prairie hen.

When they camped that night, Sacajawea learned that the interpreters—and the "interpretress"—had some special privileges. Sacajawea and Pompey, Charbonneau, and Drewyer were allowed to sleep inside a tent with the captains. The rest of the crew slept wrapped up in blankets around the fire outside.

Two nights later, when the Corps stopped to camp, Sacajawea surprised the men with some wild artichokes she had found. She had noticed a pile of driftwood that looked like a place where mice stored the roots they collected. When she dug up the dirt around the driftwood, she uncovered enough artichokes to feed the whole camp! The men liked them so much, Captain Lewis wrote about them in his journal. He even described how Sacajawea had found them.

Wherever the group camped, Sacajawea gathered healthful roots, berries, or vegetables to add to their meal. The white men marveled at her ability to find things to eat that they couldn't even see. She never forgot how her mother had taught her to seek out nutritious plants, no matter how hidden they were!

Sometimes Sacajawea walked on the riverbank beside the boats, carrying Pompey and gathering berries as she went. When she looked out across the wide plain she could see thousands of buffalo, elk, and antelope. The white men were amazed that these huge herds grazed together so peacefully! The tame animals sometimes came right up to the crew. When they stopped to hunt one day, a buffalo calf unexpectedly adopted Captain Lewis. The calf wouldn't leave Lewis's side until he got into his boat!

Just before they reached the Yellowstone River, the expedition came to a creek where Charbonneau had camped earlier with some Indian hunting parties. Since Charbonneau had been there before, the captains named the creek after him.

Three weeks after they started out, the Corps

reached the point where the Yellowstone River meets the Missouri, on the border of what is now North Dakota and Montana. Captain Lewis wrote in his journal that they were "much pleased at having arrived at this long wished for spot." The crew was so happy they decided to celebrate and everyone was given a drink. Lewis wrote, "This soon produced the fiddle and they spent the evening with much hilarity, singing, and dancing."

The Missouri River was now heading west. Sacajawea saw bighorn sheep leaping along the steep river banks. The sight must have brought memories of her childhood, when the Shoshoni men easily caught these nimble animals in the shining mountains, and the women made robes from the sheep's skin. As they traveled, Sacajawea looked for signs of Shoshoni who might be near.

One evening, disaster struck the white pirogue that Sacajawea and Pompey were riding in. Usually Drewyer steered this boat, but he was out hunting, so Charbonneau was sitting at the rudder. The Frenchman was an inexperienced sailor who was afraid of the water, and he had nearly overturned one boat already. But, near-sighted Cruzatte, the crew's best boatman, was on board, so the boat seemed to be in good hands.

Then a sudden wind hit the sails hard! Charbonneau panicked and turned the rudder the wrong way, and the wind pulled the boat over on its side. The white pirogue held all of the captains' papers and books, their instruments and medicine, and most of the trade goods for the Indians. If these things were lost, the Corps would probably have to turn back.

Both captains were on the shore. They began firing their guns and calling out orders, but no one could hear them. The boat was too far away and the roaring waves were too loud. Captain Lewis threw down his gun and began unbuttoning his coat. He was about to dive into the river when he realized he would drown in the high waves. All he and Clark could do was stand on the shore watching help-lessly.

The pirogue was on its side for thirty seconds before the crew managed to pull in the sails. By the time they got upright again, it was nearly full of water. The boat was nine hundred feet from shore, and if it sank, everyone would drown, including baby Pompey! Sacajawea sat bravely and quietly in the tossing pirogue. Charbonneau, who couldn't swim, began crying and begging to be saved!

Cruzatte ordered Charbonneau to take hold of the rudder again. The timid Frenchman sat blub-bering until Cruzatte threatened to shoot him if he didn't grab the rudder and help guide the boat.

Cruzatte told some of the men to start bailing water with the cooking kettles and ordered the others to start rowing toward the shore. There was so much confusion and shouting, no one noticed that many of the supplies had washed out of the boat. Sitting in water up to her waist, Sacajawea leaned out over the side of the boat and calmly picked up as many items as she could.

Thanks to Cruzatte's steadiness, the boat made

it safely to shore, and Sacajawea's quick thinking saved most of the important supplies. Only a little of the medicine was ruined, and some gunpowder was lost. The captains were impressed by Sacajawea's bravery. Lewis wrote in his journal that she had "equal fortitude and resolution with any person onboard at the time of the accident."

A few days later, the expedition came to a "handsome" river about five miles past the Musselshell River, and the captains named it after Sacajawea. Knowing Sacajawea meant "Bird Woman" in Minnetaree, they called it Bird Woman's River. Today this small river is called Crooked Creek.

Toward the end of May, the Corps was closer to the mountains. The Missouri River was swifter now, and the current could overturn a boat if it struck a hidden rock. To keep the boats moving along safely, some of the men walked on the shore, pulling the boats with elk skin ropes, while others stood in the boats, guiding with poles. The riverbanks often became steep and rocky, so that the men towing had to walk in the river—sometimes up to their armpits. The mud was so thick it pulled off their moccasins, and the sharp rocks cut their feet.

In this territory, danger came quickly and at any moment. One night a buffalo accidently ran through the camp. The confused bull charged right at the tent where Sacajawea and Pompey were sleeping. Luckily, Captain Lewis's big black dog, Scannon, chased it away. By the time everyone had woken up and grabbed a rifle, the beast was gone!

The next morning they found its hoof prints just inches away from where the men had been sleeping near the fire! Scannon had proved to be a good watchdog, indeed.

The Corps wondered if they should expect danger from the Indians. They hadn't seen any since the expedition had left Fort Mandan. The captains were relying on Sacajawea to find signs of Shoshoni. They found a village with 126 lodges, but it had been empty for two weeks. Sacajawea examined some moccasins that had been left there. She thought they were Atsina, allies of her people's enemies, the Blackfeet.

Soon they reached the river the Indians called the "River That Scolds at All Others." The captains had misunderstood the Minnetarees' directions and didn't know this river would be here. Now they were confused. Which river was the Missouri?

They remembered that the Indians had also told them about the Great Falls of the Missouri. The captains decided to camp and explore both rivers. Whichever river the Great Falls were on would be the Missouri. They also thought this would be a good place to bury the red pirogue and some supplies they wouldn't need right away. They would pick them up on the return trip.

The men were happy to give their cut feet and bruised shoulders a rest. They had been pulling the boats for days. Besides, their cloth shirts and pants were ragged and worn out, and they needed to make new clothing. They had learned how to make leather clothing and moccasins from the Indians at

Fort Mandan. Sacajawea must have been amazed to see these white men doing women's work with no complaining!

Each of the captains explored one of the rivers. Lewis took the River That Scolds at All Others. Before long he realized it went north, instead of west to the ocean. So he named it Maria's River, after a dear friend. It is still called that today.

It didn't take Clark long, either, to decide that the river he was on did continue west. It had to be the Missouri. Just to be sure, the captains decided Lewis should go up to the Great Falls.

It took him a day to reach them. He could hear the roar of the falls even when he was still miles away from them! He wrote that he could see the spray from the falling water "arise above the plain like a column of smoke." When he finally stood on a cliff overlooking them, he thought they were "the grandest sight I ever beheld."

To his astonishment, there was not just one, but a whole group of huge waterfalls! The largest one was nine hundred feet wide and one hundred feet high. One was like a smooth sheet of glass, while another was like thick white foam, churning down through the rocks.

Immediately Lewis sent a messenger to Clark telling him this was indeed the real Missouri and that he should bring the rest of the expedition. Lewis wanted to explore farther, then meet them back at the falls. Little did he suspect that he would find four more groups of falls over the next ten miles. Today, the city of Great Falls, Montana, is named for these magnificent waterfalls. But the "grandest sight" Captain Lewis ever beheld is gone now, destroyed by the construction of electrical power dams.

Back at camp, Sacajawea had suddenly become very ill. She had a high fever and terrible intestinal pains. Captain Clark cut open one of her veins and let her bleed for a short while. Bleeding was a common practice then. It was supposed to get rid of poisons in the body. The bleeding, however, didn't seem to help. For four days, she grew worse. Sometimes she was out of her head and raving with fever, and others had to take care of Pompey. The whole camp was worried!

Captain Clark knew that in her condition it was dangerous for her to travel, but when he heard from Captain Lewis, he had no choice: the crew must move on. The men made her as comfortable as they could in one of the boats, but this part of the river was full of rapid spots. The tossing and rolling of the boats made her feel even worse. Clark went to his supply of medicines and tried different remedies, but two days later, when they reached the falls, Sacajawea was still no better.

When Captain Lewis saw Sacajawea so sick, he was not only worried about her, but about Pompey as well. The infant was only four months old and still nursing. How would the men be able to feed and care for him? And without Sacajawea, how could they speak with the Shoshoni? They had to be able to communicate with the Indians, in order to get horses to ride over the great mountains that lay ahead. If she died, their only hope for horses would die too!

Not knowing what else to do, Lewis gave Sacajawea some mineral water he had brought back from a sulpher spring. It was like a miracle! The remedy seemed to help right away. Her fever and pain quickly disappeared, and the next day she was able to eat some buffalo soup and a little meat. The crisis seemed to be over. Nevertheless, Lewis thought Sacajawea should take more mineral water treatments. In addition, he gave Charbonneau firm instructions about what she should eat. Sacajawea was stronger, but she needed to be watched carefully.

A couple of days later, Sacajawea ate some dried fish and unripe white apples. Immediately, she had a fever again! Lewis was furious with Charbonneau. Both captains were so worried about Sacajawea they reported on her condition every day in their journals. On that day an angry Lewis wrote, "I rebuked Charbonneau severely for suffering her to indulge herself in such food." He had expected the irresponsible Frenchman to look after his wife better than this!

Sacajawea gradually improved, much to everyone's relief—and joy. They all knew how important she was to the expedition. What's more, they were all beginning to develop feelings of affection toward her.

# FINDING THE THREE FORKS

Sacajawea was well again, and it was time for the Corps to move on. Lewis's discovery of the Great Falls was one of the most spectacular discoveries the expedition had made. Unfortunately, it also presented a new problem: the boats would never be able to get up the falls! But after scouting the area for several days, Captain Clark found a land route around the great waterfalls. The route was eighteen miles long, and fairly level. Unfortunately, most of the ground was covered with prickly pear cactus.

All of the gear that the party brought with them now had to be carried over land—including the boats. The crew built a wagon from a platform they made out of logs. Then they fashioned wheels out of tree trunks so that they could roll their equipment instead of carrying it. Even so, the load was so heavy that the men had to grab on to the grass and rocks at almost every step as they pulled themselves along. The sharp prickly pear underfoot poked right through their new moccasins, even though they were made with two soles of tough buffalo hide. Before long, all the men were limping with sore feet.

To make matters worse, sudden rain storms turned the ground into sticky mud. During one cloudburst they were pounded with hailstones as big as goose eggs.

One day a black storm cloud rolled across the sky as Sacajawea and Charbonneau were walking with Captain Clark near the river. They quickly took shelter under a rock ledge in a gully. A moment later, a torrent of rain came down. The men laid down their guns and bullet pouches and sat to wait out the storm. Sacajawea took Pompey out of his cradleboard so he could stretch his little legs.

Suddenly, they heard the rumbling of a flash flood rolling toward them. They had to get out of the gully fast! Sacajawea grabbed up Pompey just as the water swept away his cradleboard. Charbonneau was so frightened he froze. Then he scrambled up the hill without his gun.

Captain Clark began pushing Sacajawea up the hill in front of him. The water rose so fast it was up to his waist before he could start climbing. By the time they reached safety, the rushing water below them was fifteen feet deep, carrying trees and rocks and everything else in its path.

They were lucky to be alive. Sacajawea, still weak from her illness, was wet and shivering. Captain Clark was afraid she would become ill again. He gave her a strong drink right there and hurried everyone back to camp.

It took the Corps more than three weeks to carry everything around the Great Falls. But by mid-July, they were on the river again. Before them in the distance were the Rocky Mountains.

Sacajawea was the only one who had ever seen these beautiful towering mountain ranges that she described as the shining mountains. The rest of the crew had been awaiting this exciting moment. Imagine how they felt when they first saw this magnificent sight! The jagged mountains were covered with snow, and the sunlight sparkled on their white tops.

The expedition passed through a place that truly dazzled them. Here, the cliffs along the river rose straight up for over a thousand feet! Captain Lewis could barely contain his excitement. He wrote, "The river appears to have forced its way through this immense body of solid rock. I called it the Gates of the Rocky Mountains!"

In the valley, sunflowers, wild cucumber, and other summer flowers were in full bloom. Even the pesky prickly pear flower looked beautiful. There were so many cactus plants, though, that the crew sometimes couldn't find enough space to lie down and sleep. One night, Captain Clark pulled seventeen prickly pear thorns out of his feet.

Because they knew they would soon need horses, the crew were on the lookout for signs of Indians as they paddled along the river. One day they came across several abandoned Indian camps. A few days later, they spotted smoke in the distance coming from burning prairie fires. It looked as though the Indians were warning one another that white men were coming. On another day the men were excited to find fresh horse tracks going toward the mountains.

Sacajawea began to recognize certain things about the land around her. First there was the thrilling, familiar sight of the beautiful mountains she had left behind years ago. And now she could smell the sagebrush, too. She found the yellow and purple currants and fuzzy red choke cherries she remembered gathering as a child. She sensed that the expedition was close to her people's buffalo hunting grounds. They were on the plain where "three rivers flowed into one." This was the Three Forks area of southwestern Montana where the Missouri is formed by three separate rivers.

Memories of her childhood must have come flooding back to Sacajawea. Charbonneau became annoyed with her because she seemed so lost in her thoughts. One day when he caught her staring off at the prairie, he lost his temper and slapped her! Fortunately, Captain Clark happened to be there at the time, and he told the Frenchman that he would not tolerate Charbonneau striking Sacajawea again!

As they moved closer to the mountains, Captain Lewis worried that the river would become rocky or that they would come to another set of falls. Sacajawea told him she knew this river and that it would not change or become dangerous. And she was right! Three days later, on July 28, 1805, they came safely to the Three Forks.

The Corps made camp right at the place where Sacajawea and her family had been camped when the Minnetarees captured her. With Charbonneau translating, she told the men how she and her people had been captured by the Minnetarees. She

40

described to them how she had run for three miles up the widest of the three forks, hidden in the woods, and watched as many of her people were killed.

Sacajawea pointed out the spot where she had been grabbed up as she had tried to cross the river. That terrible moment had changed her whole life, but Sacajawea did not show her feelings about that fateful day. As a Shoshoni, she had been taught that it was weak and childish to act in an emotional way.

Captain Lewis thought it was odd that Sacajawea was not sad or upset as she told her painful story. He decided that her capture hadn't been so painful for her. In his journal, he wrote, "If she has enough to eat and a few trinkets to wear, I believe she would be perfectly content anywhere." But he would soon find out how wrong he was.

The captains named the three forks of the rivers they had found the Jefferson, Madison, and Gallatin rivers, after three of the most important political leaders of the time. The widest one was called the Jefferson, after the president. Sacajawea had followed the Jefferson when she ran to escape the Minnetarees. Now the Corps followed it toward the mountains.

After they had traveled a few days along the river, Sacajawea looked up from her boat and pointed out a tall rock on a high plain. She said the Shoshoni called it Beaver's Head Rock because it looked like that familiar animal to them. To her, Beaver's Head Rock meant that they were near the pass where her people crossed the mountains each year in search of food. If her memory served her well, the Shoshoni village was on a river in the valley just beyond the pass.

Sacajawea told the captains that to find her people, they should follow the Jefferson River until it divided. Then they should take the fork that went west. The Shoshoni would either be on the Jefferson River, or on the west fork. Then she showed them an Indian road beside the river. It was the road her people took back and forth from the mountains to the plains.

When Lewis heard this, he decided to cross the mountains immediately. He declared that he was determined to find the Shoshoni—or other Indians who would sell them horses—even if it took him a month. Clark would follow with the supplies.

The next day—leaving Clark, Sacajawea, and the rest of the party in camp—Lewis and three crew members, Drewyer, Shields, and McNeal, took off on foot, down the Shoshoni road. When they came to the place where the Jefferson divided, the road split also, and they took the fork that had fresh horse tracks on it. Lewis left a note on a willow pole telling Captain Clark which way he and his men had gone. He asked Clark to wait at this spot for him to return, then he set off to find the Shoshoni in their mountain retreat. No one knows why Captain Lewis did not take Sacajawea with him. If he had, his first encounter with the Shoshoni might have been easier.

# LOOKING FOR SHOSHONI

Now that Sacajawea had told him that the Shoshoni were near, Captain Lewis was positive he'd find them soon. Sure enough, the next day when he was taking a walk he spotted an Indian on a horse about two miles away, heading toward him. Lewis looked through his telescope at the rider. He could see that the man was short and dark like Sacajawea and that he was dressed differently from any tribe Lewis had seen. This must be a Shoshoni!

When the two men were about a mile apart, Lewis made a sign of friendship that Sacajawea had taught him. Three times he waved a blanket over his head, then lowered it to the ground. To show he was peaceful, he even put his gun down on the ground.

The Indian kept looking over his shoulder at Drewyer and Shields. They had started out earlier to scout around. Now they were walking toward the Indian from two sides. Lewis didn't want to frighten the Indian by calling out to his men. Instead he shouted, *"Tab ba bone!"* Sacajawea had taught him this Shoshoni word, which meant "outsider," or "white man."

*"Tab ba bone!"* Lewis called out again. Then he

rolled up his sleeve to show a part of his arm that hadn't been tanned by the sun and was still pale skin. But the Indian began backing up.

Lewis finally signaled his men to stop! Drewyer froze immediately, but Shields kept coming. Lewis was only a hundred feet away when the Indian wheeled his horse around. Lewis's heart sank as he watched the Indian rider disappear into the willow brush. He was furious with Shields, who later said that he hadn't seen the signal.

The next morning the men saw a small group of Indians who also ran away. Lewis tried to catch the Indians' dogs and tie beads around their necks as gifts, but the dogs couldn't be caught.

Later that day, the explorers walked around a large rock. To their surprise, they found themselves face to face with four Indian women! The two young women ran away, but an old woman and child couldn't escape. They knelt down on the ground and bowed their heads.

The old woman was shocked when Lewis tenderly lifted her up. After she called the others back, he gave them all gifts of blue beads and mirrors. Then he put red paint on their faces, another sign of peace. The four women agreed to take the friendly white men to their camp.

The party had walked about two miles when sixty warriors rode up at full speed! Captain Lewis and his men were outnumbered. As a sign of peace, they threw down their guns and held up the American flag. Just then, the women ran to their leader, speaking excitedly and showing him their gifts. What were they telling him, Lewis wondered. He had no idea what the Indians would do.

To Lewis's surprise, the leader leaped off his horse and hugged the captain! The leader and two warriors solemnly rubbed cheeks with Lewis, leaving paint on his face. Then the rest of the Indians climbed down from their horses to hug and rub faces. Soon everyone had paint on their cheeks.

Lewis brought out the peace pipe. Everyone sat in a circle and the Indians took off their moccasins. This was a sign of sincerity, which meant "May I always go barefoot if I lie to you." Going barefoot in this harsh land full of prickly pears would be a real hardship—as the white men already knew.

To Captain Lewis's joy, the Indians were, indeed, Shoshoni. Their leader's name was Cameahwait. He wore a beautiful cape, called a tippit. It was made of hundreds of tiny ermine skins. The collar was a whole otter skin, including the head and tail, and was decorated with shells. Other men had on collars made of bear claws.

Most of the warriors wore leather shirts, leggings, and moccasins, fringed and decorated with colored porcupine quills. Many had tied beads and eagle feathers in their hair and some wore headbands of otter skin.

Drewyer did his best to interpret for Captain Lewis and Cameahwait with sign language. Cameahwait said his party was on its way to their buffalo hunting grounds on the plains. His scouts had told

him of the white men's arrival. The Shoshoni had never seen a white man before.

They had been afraid that the explorers were friends of the Minnetarees, their enemies. The Minnetarees had raided their village in the spring, killing twenty Shoshoni warriors and taking prisoners and horses. Cameahwait's hair was cut very short, which was a Shoshoni way of showing grief. He was mourning for his friends who had died fighting the Minnetarees.

Lewis explained through Drewyer that he had been sent in peace by the "Great White Father," President Jefferson. He gave out presents and an American flag. After the two groups got to know each other better, the Shoshoni took the white men to their camp.

When they arrived, Lewis passed out presents to the women and children who had all crowded around to look at the white men. Lewis noticed that the women's elk-skin dresses were also decorated with designs woven from porcupine quills and colored beads. Although beads were popular, only the children wore necklaces made of them.

About four hundred people lived in this camp, and several hundred horses grazed close by. The Shoshoni lived in tepees made of willow branches. The Minnetarees had burned all but one of their leather tepees during their spring raid. It would take them many months of hunting to get enough skins to make more.

Cameahwait took the explorers to the leather tepee for a friendship ceremony. They sat on willow branches with antelope skins thrown over them. This time the white men took off their moccasins, too. The Indians pulled up a circle of grass from the center of the lodge and made a special fire inside of it. Cameahwait lit the peace pipe from the fire then pointed the pipe to the east, west, south, and north.

The chief handed the pipe to Captain Lewis, then pulled it back. He pointed the pipe up to the heavens and down toward the fire. Three times Cameahwait did this. Each time he offered it, he took it back, then pointed it up and down. After the third time, he let Lewis have the pipe and everyone had a smoke.

All that the Indians could offer the white men to eat were cakes made of dried choke cherries. They apologized because they had no other food, but they could dance for their guests! The Indians entertained the white men for hours! By midnight, Lewis was so tired he couldn't stay up any longer and left the party.

The next day, Lewis asked Cameahwait to come meet the rest of his crew. They could bring the expedition's supplies back to camp to trade for horses. Lewis told Cameahwait that a Shoshoni woman was traveling with them. He wanted the chief to meet Sacajawea, who could translate his words to Cameahwait better than Drewyer's sign language. At first Cameahwait said he would go, but then he changed his mind. Some of his warriors were afraid of a trap, he said.

Lewis challenged the leader: Was anyone brave

enough to go and find out the truth, he asked? Cameahwait said fiercely that he, for one, was not afraid! But only eight braves volunteered to go with him.

As Cameahwait left, some of the women began to sob and wail. By the time the party had gone a few miles, however, nearly all the warriors had joined them—and most of the women, too.

As they approached the meeting place, the Indians stopped. Cameahwait was still afraid of a trap. He gave Lewis and his men fur tippets to wear, so that they would look like Indians from a distance. Now Lewis couldn't let the expedition attack the group, because he and his men would be killed, too. Lewis, realizing why Cameahwait was afraid, gave him his hat so that the Indian would be taken for a white man if they were attacked.

When they arrived at the two forks of the Jefferson River, Captain Clark wasn't there. The Indians became nervous again. Lewis gave his gun to Cameahwait. If there was an ambush, he said, the leader could shoot him. At that point, Lewis remembered the note he had left for Clark! He had Drewyer bring it to him. Then he pretended it was from Clark saying he was on his way.

Cameahwait seemed satisfied with the letter, but that night Lewis didn't sleep very well. If the Indians lost trust in him and left, they would hide in the mountains and warn other bands not to help the Corps of Discovery. If that happened, the expedition would never get the horses it needed.

What was worse, if Cameahwait decided this was a trap, he might even kill them!

Captain Lewis was lucky. That very next morning, an Indian scout saw Captain Clark, Sacajawea, and Charbonneau. Cameahwait was delighted with this news and hugged Lewis. But he kept the captain with him while he sent out a small greeting party with Drewyer dressed like an Indian.

Drewyer's costume confused Clark. Sacajawea, however, knew exactly who these people were! As the greeting party came closer, her face lit up with joy and she began to dance. She placed her fingers in her mouth—a sign to show Clark that these were her people—then ran to meet them.

As Clark watched Sacajawea in amazement, Drewyer ran up to him and told him quickly what had happened. When the rest of Clark's party caught up, everyone hurried back to Captain Lewis and Cameahwait. As they walked along, the Indians sang loudly and happily!

# LITTLE BIRD RETURNS

As the expedition entered the Shoshoni camp, the Indians gathered around them. Suddenly, a young woman pushed through the crowd toward Sacajawea. It was her childhood friend who had also been captured by the Minnetarees. Sacajawea couldn't believe her eyes! They held each other tightly, crying softly.

Years ago, the two friends had shared their hardships and sadness when they were prisoners in the Minnetaree camp. After her friend had run away, Sacajawea never knew if she was alive or dead. It was such a long way back to the Shoshoni village from the Minnetaree camp. It didn't seem possible to Sacajawea that her friend could have made it.

Sacajawea's friend never thought she would see her companion again, either. But there she was, standing right in front of her with a beautiful baby son! The friends from days gone by had a million questions to ask each other.

In the meantime, other women crowded around Sacajawea, hugging and talking excitedly. She went from one to another, searching for familiar faces. Once again, she was speaking the language of her childhood! Many things were familiar—the way her people walked and dressed and the way their camp smelled. Her family! Were they here? It was too late to ask. Someone had just sent for her; she was needed at council.

The leaders had gathered in a nearby tent. After everyone took off their moccasins, they smoked the peace pipe. Captain Clark was presented to Cameahwait. He seated Clark on a white robe and tied six small shells in the captain's red hair. These sea shells were very valuable to the Shoshoni. Giving them to Clark was a great sign of friendship.

In a solemn ceremony, Cameahwait gave his own name to Captain Clark. This was an honor because names were very important to the Shoshoni. The men of the tribe had several names—only one of which was used in war. This was because they believed that they would lose their strength if an enemy heard their real name. Giving Clark his real name was a sign of Cameahwait's sincerity and respect. From then on, the captain was called Cameahwait by the Shoshoni.

Sacajawea entered the tepee and sat down. As an interpreter, she was an important person at the council. But it must have felt strange to her to be there. Women were allowed to watch council, but never to talk. She *must* speak now, though. The expedition depended on her to help them get horses and guides for the trip west.

When Cameahwait began to speak, Sacajawea stared at him for a moment. Suddenly, she jumped up and threw her blanket over his shoulder. Cameahwait was her brother! He was alive! Sacajawea couldn't hold back her tears.

At first, Cameahwait was bewildered. He didn't know who she was. Then he realized it was his younger sister, Little Bird, whom he had thought was captured and lost forever! He did his best not to weep, too—especially in front of the white men. But the council could tell how moved he was.

Everyone waited while Sacajawea and Cameahwait spoke quietly with each other for a few minutes. Sacajawea sat down again to interpret, but she was too overcome with happiness and kept bursting into tears. The captains understood what this day meant to her, and they let her take her time at council. Lewis now realized how wrong he had been to think that Sacajawea didn't care about finding her people.

Lewis and Clark gave gifts to all those present. Several other Indian leaders were given medals with President Jefferson's face stamped on them. One of them received a uniform coat and a pair of red pants. Lewis passed out red paint, moccasins, tobacco, and looking glasses. The Indians were especially fond of beads, and they were very happy to get metal knives.

Then the discussions began. The translation went through four languages. First the captains spoke to Drewyer in English, then he repeated what they said to Charbonneau in French, then Charbonneau conversed with Sacajawea in Minnetaree. From Minnetaree Sacajawea translated into Shoshoni.

Through Sacajawea, the captains told the Indians that the United States now owned this land.

Their Great White Father, President Jefferson, wanted to trade with them for furs. In turn, the Shoshoni could get many useful things from the United States, including food. In order to set up this trade, the Great Father's messengers needed the Shoshoni's help. They needed horses to get across the mountains.

Cameahwait said he didn't have any horses to spare, but he would send someone to his people's village over the mountains and ask them to bring horses. Even though Cameahwait was an important Shoshoni leader, he couldn't order his people to sell their horses. A Shoshoni leader could only advise his people or suggest that they do something.

After the council, Cameahwait told Sacajawea what had happened to her family. It was sad news. All but Cameahwait, her older brother, and her sister's small son had been killed on that fateful day when they had been ambushed by the Minnetarees.

As Sacajawea spoke with Cameahwait, Lewis and Clark continued to make friends with their Shoshoni hosts. Corn did not grow in the Pacific Northwest at that time, and the captains took great pleasure in giving the Shoshoni their first taste of corn meal, which the Indians thought was absolutely delicious! Sacajawea brought out the sugar lump she had been saving for Pompey. She gave it Cameahwait, who had never eaten sugar. He swore it was the best food he had ever tasted.

After all the ceremonies were finished, Sacajawea and Charbonneau rode over to Cameahwait's village to help trade for the horses. Clark traveled with them to the village, then went exploring to decide which route the expedition should take next. He took an old Indian man named Toby as his guide.

They went quite a distance up through the mountains, following the Salmon River. Clark soon realized the mountains were too rugged to cross, and the river too wild for their boats. He figured the expedition would have to go farther north before they could cross the mountains. He sent a rider to Lewis with a letter telling him this.

Back at camp, Lewis and the rest of the crew buried more of their supplies. They couldn't carry everything over the mountains, so they would have to store part of their gear here. Lewis did not leave their provisions with the Shoshoni, fearing that the Indians would use them. Instead the crew dug their hole in secret and sneaked out at night to bury their supplies.

Using sign language, Lewis asked Cameahwait to describe the land to the west. Cameahwait made a map on the ground for Lewis. He made mountains with piles of sand and drew the rivers that flowed around them. Then he told Lewis about the Nez Percé or "pierced nose" Indians who wore bones and other ornaments in their noses. The Nez Percé crossed the mountains every year through a northern pass. Their trail, he said, was rocky and covered with fallen trees and there was nothing to hunt. The Nez Percé went hungry all the way through the pass.

But if Indian women and children can make it

through this pass every year, Lewis thought, so can the Corps of Discovery. He'd discuss using this northern pass with Clark as soon as he returned.

Within a few days, Sacajawea and Charbonneau returned with more than fifty Indians from Cameahwait's village. Lewis was able to purchase nine horses and a mule from them. For three horses, he paid an ax, a knife, a handkerchief, and some paint. The mule was a stronger pack animal and more expensive. It cost two knives, some handkerchiefs, a shirt, and leggings.

They still needed more horses. Lewis decided to go back to the village himself to try to get more. Since the expedition didn't have enough horses to carry all their supplies, he asked Cameahwait if he could hire Indian women to carry the rest. Cameahwait said yes, promising his people would help Lewis get back to the village.

Lewis had bought a horse for Sacajawea. As they set out, she was the only member of the expedition allowed to ride. This was a strange sight to the Shoshoni because Indian women only rode if there were enough horses for everyone. If there weren't, the men rode while the women walked and carried the baggage, as well.

To make Sacajawea the only rider was a way Lewis could honor her. But it was probably insulting to the Shoshoni women who were carrying the provisions, causing them to resent her.

The next morning, Sacajawea discovered that Cameahwait had changed his mind. He was not going to help carry the expedition's supplies back to his village. He was taking his people to their buffalo hunting grounds, instead.

Cameahwait's people were hungry. Every day they spent with the Corps was another day without food. Sacajawea knew what it was like to be hungry like that. But she also knew that if Cameahwait left, the expedition would be stuck in the mountains with all their baggage and no way to buy horses!

Sacajawea went to Charbonneau, told him the news, and said he should let the captains know immediately. Her husband didn't think her news was so important, though, and waited until that afternoon to tell Lewis. Lewis couldn't believe Charbonneau was so foolish! He scolded the Frenchman for waiting all day to tell him something of such great importance to the expedition.

Lewis called the Shoshoni leaders together right away. He said he had shared his food with them, and his government had promised to protect them. Could they not trust him? He had trusted them when Cameahwait said they would help. Why had they lied to him?

Two of the leaders said it was Cameahwait's decision, not theirs. Cameahwait sat silently for a few moments. Finally, he spoke. It hurt him to see his people hungry. That was why he had changed his plan. But he had been wrong and would keep his promise now.

The party set out again through the mountains. When they reached Cameahwait's village, Lewis found Clark's letter waiting for him. He was happy to read that his friend also thought a northern route, like the one followed by the Nez Percé, would be better.

It took several days of hard bargaining, but Lewis finally purchased twenty-nine horses. Clark wrote in his journal that the expedition now had enough animals to ride and carry supplies—"and to eat, if necessary!" The Corps was ready to go through the mountains. Cameahwait had agreed to ride with them part of the way to the northern mountain pass.

It was time for Sacajawea to leave her people once again. Should she stay this time? She had missed the ways of her childhood, but nearly all her family were dead, and things were different now. She was different, too. She had been a child when she left, but now she had her own child and a husband. She had lived in other places and learned new ways. These new ways gave her and Pompey enough food and warm clothing. The faces of her people had reminded her of how hard their nomadic life was.

She decided to go on with the Corps of Discovery and her husband. It was hard to say goodbye to her brothers and friends, and she hated to leave her dead sister's son. Surely they would meet again when the expedition returned. Or was she leaving them this time, forever?

# THE PACIFIC OCEAN

On September 2, 1805, the expedition headed north, traveling up what is now the border between Idaho and Montana. The underbrush was so thick on the rocky hillsides, they had to hack a trail through it. With their horses stumbling and falling, they only covered five miles before dark.

The next morning two inches of snow fell, and it began to rain and sleet! The horses kept sliding down the steep icy mountainsides. Captain Clark wrote, "Our horses were in perpetual danger of slipping to their certain destruction." He thought that this trail was made up of "some of the worst roads that ever horses passed." Already, some of them were too lame to go on.

On the third day the expedition was relieved to meet some friendly Flathead Indians who gave them food to eat and sold them fresh horses. The crew was amazed by the Flathead's strange language. These Indians made a kind of gurgling sound when they spoke. Sacajawea couldn't understand these people either, even though she knew some Flathead tribes. The Corps stayed with them for a day just so Captain Lewis could describe them in his journal.

The Corps crossed the Bitterroot River a week after they had started out. When Toby, the old Shoshoni guide, told them they were near the Nez

Percé pass, the captains decided to rest a day before starting through. They named their camp Traveller's Rest.

In order to reach the pass, the expedition climbed to a trail high in the mountains. The Nez Percé later named it Lolo Pass, and that is what it is called today. For three days the crew and their horses stumbled up and down the rugged hills and hollows heading toward the pass, climbing over trees that had fallen across the trail. For one whole day, they couldn't find any water.

When the expedition finally came over the pass, they found themselves on a firm, level road. It turned west along a river called the Kooskooskee, now named the Clearwater. But they weren't out of the mountains yet. The road went up again, winding in every direction.

They had nothing to eat now except berries and a little cornmeal. Captain Clark had been right when he said they might have to eat some of their horses. A young horse was killed to feed the crew, and the captains named a nearby stream Colt Killed Creek.

Snow began falling, and in one day it was knee deep. Captain Clark wrote, "I have been wet and as cold in every part as I ever was in my life. Indeed, I was at one time fearful my feet would freeze in the thin moccasins I wore." That night they had to kill a second horse for food.

It took them several more freezing wet days to get through the mountains. They were cold, hungry, and exhausted, but they made it. The Indians were right; there was no river flowing through the mountains, as President Jefferson had hoped. But the expedition had found the pass that connected the rivers on either side of the mountains. This was a momentous discovery. Now they would find a way to travel across the whole country—a way that would lead to an epic-making chapter in American history: the opening of the west.

Finally, the Corps came to a large village of the Nez Percé. They fed the Corps dried salmon and camas root. The men weren't used to this diet and most of them were already ill from "mountain fever," caused by being in a high, cold altitude. The food gave everyone diarrhea and stomach cramps. Captain Clark described their pitiful condition in his journal. "Captain Lewis scarcely able to ride on a gentle horse. Several men so unwell that they were compelled to lie on the side of the road for some time." Clark had to admit that he, too, was "a little unwell."

The Nez Percé were kind and generous, and the expedition stayed with them for two weeks. During that time they developed a strong friendship with their chief, Twisted Hair. Through sign language, Twisted Hair told the captains that the Kooskooskee River was safe for boats. Then the Indians taught the explorers a quick way to make dugout canoes. They burned out the hollow of a log, instead of hacking it.

Using this method, the men had five boats ready in just a few days. Then they branded their thirty-eight horses, which the Nez Percé had agreed to look after until the expedition returned the following spring. Saddles and some gunpowder were buried, along with other supplies they would pick up on their way back. On October 7, 1805, the Corps was ready to go again—this time to descend the Columbia River.

Twisted Hair and his brother, Chief Tetoharsky, offered to accompany their new friends down the Kooskooskee River to the Columbia. It was lucky they did, because Toby and his son had left. The Shoshoni guides were in such a hurry to leave, they didn't even bother to get their pay! Probably, they wanted to get home before winter snow blocked their route and left them stranded in hostile territory.

The Kooskooskee met the Kimooenin River on the border of what is now Idaho and Washington. The town of Lewistown was later built at that spot, and the Kimooenin River is now called the Snake River. Along the way, different Indian groups traveled with the Corps on the river banks. One group of local people would help them for a while, then another would take over. Twisted Hair and Tetoharsky often went on ahead of the expedition to assure villages that the white men following them could be trusted.

On October 16, 1805, six months after they had left Fort Mandan, the expedition came to the Columbia River, part of which forms the border between the present-day states of Washington and Oregon. It was an important moment, but the brave group of explorers didn't feel much like celebrating. They had to reach the Pacific Ocean before cold weather set in. And before they got there, they still had many more miles of wild, rough rivers to travel and the Columbia gorge to pass through.

The men's spirits rose when they saw an Indian wearing a sailor's jacket coming toward them. He must have gotten the jacket from traders on the Pacific Ocean. This was a sign that they were getting closer to their goal: the mouth of the Columbia River.

A few days later, when Captain Clark was traveling ahead of the Corps with three other men, he came to an Indian village. He was surprised when all the Indians there ran from him. He entered one of the lodges and saw about thirty men, women, and children huddled together. When he offered them the peace pipe, they became upset. Finally, he sat on a rock and put out some gifts for the villagers. Still no one would come out. Why were these Indians so afraid of him?

The rest of the Corps eventually caught up with Clark. As soon as the Indians saw Sacajawea, they all came out of their lodges. They were afraid of Clark because they had never seen white people before and thought that he would harm them. The sight of Sacajawea and little Pompey, however, made them feel safe. In that area, it was an Indian custom that no woman or child ever traveled with a war party.

Continuing on their trek, the Corps reached the great Celilo Falls. Here, the river fell straight down over twenty-foot cliffs, then rushed through a narrow channel before dropping over another steep ledge. These falls were not as immense as the Great Falls, but the supplies still had to be carried around them. The crew bypassed three more rough places in the river in just a few days. They had never seen such fierce waters before. They were used to surviving in the wilderness, but they had never experienced any river like the Columbia!

After the Celilo Falls, Clark hoped that they had passed through the worst part of the Columbia. Just four days later, however, the boats came to another twenty-foot waterfall, the Cascades, which are now covered by water from the Bonneville Dam. Once again, everything had to be hauled over land.

Twisted Hair and Tetoharsky wanted to go home now. They were too near the territory of their enemies. The captains were sorry to see their friends go. The Nez Percé chiefs had helped the expedition meet the local tribes. Now only the sight of Sacajawea and Pompey would tell other Indians that these white men were friendly.

The next Indians the Corps met were the Skilloots. They had flat, sloping foreheads. When their children were born, their heads were placed between two boards. The boards were kept pressed together for about a year. This device made the baby's forehead slope back. A sloping forehead was considered a sign of beauty among the Skilloots. The captains drew pictures of this fascinating contraption and of the Skilloots' heads to send to President Jefferson.

The Skilloots gave the expedition a root called wappato, which looked like a potato. The Indians cooked the root in hot coals until it was soft. Sacajawea had never seen wappato. She was very fond of roots and she especially liked this one.

The Corps was now in the northwest part of the country, where it rains much of the time. One day heavy rain and winds made such high waves on the river that Sacajawea and many of the others became seasick. When they stopped to camp they couldn't go very far up on shore because the hills were too steep. They were forced to sleep on wet sand that was crawling with sand fleas.

A week later it was still raining so hard that no one was able to hunt. Huge trees had slid off the muddy banks and begun floating down the river. Some of them were two hundred feet long and seven feet thick. They crashed through the water, making the river too dangerous to navigate. Finally the expedition made a camp on some huge logs that were lying on the sand, but it wasn't much safer there. High tide brought the water up on the sand and caused the logs to float, tossing the sleeping crew about.

The captains were desperate to find another place to camp, so Clark took off in the downpour to explore farther inland. He could barely hack his way through the fifteen-foot-high underbrush of thorny thickets and ferns growing above the shoreline. Finally he managed to pull himself up a steep hill to look around, but it was too foggy to see very far. Frustrated, the captain returned with no solution for his drenched crew.

After twelve straight days of rain, three men braved the crashing waves to look farther down river. They came rushing back with good news. Not too far away was a beach with a safe place for the boats. On the following day the wind let up in the afternoon. The break in the weather was just what the expedition was waiting for. They loaded up the canoes in a flash and paddled furiously toward the beach.

The ocean was not far from their new camp, and Clark could not wait to take a few of the men to see the "big water." Finally they had reached their goal! As they stood looking out over the glittering expanse of ocean, he wrote that they were deeply impressed, ". . . beholding with astonishment the high waves dashing against the rocks and this immense ocean."

Their camp was visited by various Indian tribes that lived in the area. One day a Chinnook chief came wearing an otter skin robe. It was the most magnificent fur the captains had ever seen. They wanted it for President Jefferson, but the only thing the chief would trade for it was a beautiful belt of blue beads Sacajawea wore around her waist. The captains offered every piece of trade goods they had. No, the chief wanted Sacajawea's belt, and only the belt.

Blue beads were like gold among all the Indians the expedition had met, and Sacajawea's belt

was very valuable. If the belt meant something special to her, she never said. She took it off and silently handed it over. In turn, the grateful captains gave her a coat made of blue cloth. The coat was warm, but hardly as beautiful as the belt she had just given up for the Great White Father.

The expedition moved near the ocean on the north side of the Columbia River. It seemed unbelievable to them that it was still raining. "O! how horrible is the day!" Captain Clark wrote about the weather. Their leather clothes and the robes they slept under had been wet for so long, they were rotted.

What's more, there was no game or fresh water at this place. They didn't want to go too far back up the Columbia, for fear they'd miss a trade boat that might land near the river. Besides, President Jefferson was supposed to be sending a ship to meet them.

Indians told them there were plenty of deer and elk and good places to camp on the south side of the river. So, Lewis went across to see if they were right. He found a dry spot about thirty feet above the ocean. Nearby were plenty of pine trees to build a fort, and Lewis saw elk roaming in the woods.

He reported back to the Corps and gave everyone a vote on where to live. Sacajawea, concerned about finding food, voted to live where there were plenty of "pota" or wappato roots. The crew agreed to cross to the south side of the river.

# WINTER AT FORT CLATSOP

On December 7, 1805, the Corps began building their winter home. It took them a month
to finish, and it rained every day they worked. In
the meantime, they lived in damp, smoky huts.
Every morning they shook the fleas out of their
blankets, then dried their clothes. Everyone had
colds and aching joints from the wet weather.

The crew was still not used to eating dried fish
and roots, a diet that gave them constant diarrhea.
Finally, Captain Clark couldn't eat at all. Sacajawea
had a small piece of bread that she had carried all
the way from Fort Mandan. She had saved it for
Pompey, but decided Clark needed it. By now, the
bread was sour from being wet, but the Red
Headed Chief was delighted to have it. He hadn't
eaten any bread in months. Just the taste of it
heartened him, and when the hunters finally began
bringing fresh elk meat back to camp, everyone
cheered up.

The Corps soon discovered that their meat
spoiled quickly in the damp, soggy weather, especially since they had no salt to preserve it. The
seven barrels they had lugged from Fort Mandan
had been used up. Luckily, however, they were
near a perfect source of salt—the ocean. They set
up a salt works right on the beach. The ocean water

was boiled in kettles until it evaporated, leaving the salt behind.

On Christmas Day Sacajawea was awakened by the men shouting and singing and firing their guns. Sacajawea remembered that the white people exchanged gifts on this "great medicine day." This year she had her own gifts to give—twenty-four white weasel tails for Captain Clark.

The guns awoke Sacajawea again on New Year's morning, but the men were in no mood to welcome the arrival of 1806. They didn't even celebrate when they set the last log of their winter home in place that very day. Instead they sat around the fire and daydreamed about where they would be next New Year's Day.

The captains called their new home Fort Clatsop, after the Indians who lived nearby. It consisted of eight cabins built in a circle. They lived in seven of the cabins and used one for storage. The doors to the cabins all faced the center of the fort, while the back of them formed a protective wall against any Indian raids.

One day, a Clatsop chief, Comowool, brought the expedition some blubber as a gift. It came from a whale that had been stranded on the beach. Everyone thought the cooked blubber tasted as good as beaver, and they were eager for more. Clark organized a party to go find the whale. When Sacajawea discovered she was not included, she went to the captains.

She told them firmly that she had traveled all

this way with the men to see the great waters. She had been near the ocean for more than a month and still not seen it. Now there was a giant fish to see, too. She thought it would be very unfair if she weren't able to see both of them. Clark couldn't say no. Sacajawea had certainly earned the right to make the trip.

The next morning, Captain Clark hired a guide to take them to the whale. The group had walked two and a half miles when suddenly the guide stopped. He pointed ahead to the steep mountain they had to cross and said, *"Pe Shack."* That meant "bad."

With eleven-month-old Pompey on her back, Sacajawea climbed along with the men on a trail that went almost straight up. It took them two hours to go a thousand feet. That night they camped on the mountainside.

The next morning Sacajawea stood on the mountain and looked out over the Pacific Ocean. The great, blue-green waters stretched out endlessly before her, and huge white waves crashed against the rocky shore. There was water as far as her eyes could see! How far could a canoe go on this water? What was on the other shore?

By the time the party reached the whale, it was only a skeleton. The Indians had already picked it clean! However, they agreed to sell Captain Clark three hundred pounds of blubber. Sacajawea walked around the skeleton, which was more than one hundred feet long. Would anyone ever believe

her if she told them about this big fish? The Pacific Ocean must be terrifically deep and wide to hold a fish this size!

Seeing the ocean and the whale were the most exciting events that the party experienced at Fort Clatsop—except for Pompey's becoming one year old in February. Sacajawea didn't need to keep him in the cradleboard as much anymore. Now he was free to crawl around the cabin floor and take his first steps. Captain Clark adored Pompey and called him "my little dancing boy."

During the winter months, it rained every day. Life at Fort Clatsop was quiet. The captains wrote their reports for President Jefferson and put labels on the new plants and animals they had found. Clark drew maps of all the territories they had passed through, and Lewis described all the Indian tribes they had met.

All winter they waited for President Jefferson's boat to come, but the president had never sent one. He had expected Lewis and Clark to send him a message when they reached the Great Falls. When he didn't hear from them, he assumed they were dead.

Without supplies from Jefferson, they had to gather together what they could for the journey back. The men hunted, Sacajawea dug up roots and picked berries, and they all dried as much food as they could. Sacajawea boiled elk bones to get grease to use for gun oil and for making candles.

Sacajawea and the men made new clothes for the return trip, too. By spring they had almost four hundred pairs of moccasins. They also boiled sea water so that they had plenty of salt, and made sure that all their guns and boats had been repaired. Still, they didn't have many goods left over for bartering.

On March 23, 1806, the Corps gave Fort Clatsop and everything in it to Chief Comowool and started for home. They were eager to get out of that rainy place!

Traveling was even harder on the return trip because the river was swollen from melting snow. In some places the river was twenty feet deeper than it had been in the fall. After three days they had come only seven miles. The captains felt the river was too dangerous, so they bought horses from local Indians to travel by land.

It was May 4 when the Corps reached the Kooskooskee River, where they came upon Chief Tetoharsky. He said he knew of a short cut to the spot where his brother, Twisted Hair, had been keeping the Corps' horses.

Along the way, the Indians they met were all eager to see Captain Clark, who had treated a man's boil when the expedition had passed through in the fall. The man had told others how the captain had cured him, and the story had passed from village to village. Now the Indians called Clark the "great medicine man," and lined up to be healed wherever the Corps stopped. Clark ended up treating nearly forty Indians a day! His services had always been free, but now, since their trade goods were almost gone, he began to trade his doctoring for supplies and horses.

When the expedition reached Twisted Hair, all their horses were returned in fine shape. Three more Nez Percé chiefs joined the group, and the captains decided it was time for a big council. Among the Nez Percé was a Shoshoni boy who had been taken prisoner. Sacajawea, Charbonneau, and the boy translated for the council. Since there were so many chiefs, it took most of the day to complete the talks.

The Nez Percé were impressed by the white men's words and agreed to live in peace with their enemies, as the Great Father asked. After the council, several of Twisted Hair's sons said they would guide the Corps through the Rockies, but not until the mountain snows had melted.

The expedition dug up the saddles and supplies they had buried here last October on their way to the Pacific Ocean. Sacajawea gathered fennel roots and onions that grew nearby and began drying them to eat when they were crossing the mountains.

For the first time during the long, hard trip, Pompey became ill. His baby teeth were coming in, causing high fever and diarrhea. Then his jaw and throat swelled up to a frightening size. The captains gave him cream of tarter and put a dressing of wild onions on his neck.

For two days and nights, the little boy couldn't sleep. Sacajawea rocked him and sang to him until he finally dropped off. After a week, his fever was still high, and his jaw and neck seemed to get bigger every day.

The swelling finally turned into a big, painful boil. At that point Captain Clark mixed together some beeswax, bear oil, and pine needle sap to put on it. The sticky dressing dried up the boil, but it took Clark's "little dancing boy" nearly three weeks to fully recover.

It was now June and the Corps was eager to be on its way. The Nez Percé chief warned them that the snow in the mountains was still too deep to wade through. They advised the Corps to wait until the full moon in July.

The captains thought highly of the chief's advice, but they knew that they had to reach Fort Mandan before the winter ice covered the Missouri River. On June 10, they decided that they absolutely had to leave. Cut Nose promised that two young chiefs would catch up with the expedition and go with them as far as the Great Falls of the Missouri. Maybe, he said, the chiefs would even go to Washington to meet the Great Father!

But when the Corps neared Lolo Pass, where they would cross through the mountains, the young chiefs hadn't shown up yet. The captains decided not to wait for them. They didn't think they needed a guide, since they had come through the pass once before with old Toby.

Five days later, they reached the mountains and started climbing the slick, muddy trail. Soon they reached ground where the snow was ten feet deep, but luckily it was hard enough for the horses to walk on. Four miles higher, however, it was fifteen feet deep. Captain Clark, who was in front of the line, couldn't find the trees the Indians had marked to show the way. There was no way they could find grass for the horses, or wood for a fire in this snow.

Even though it was mid-June, the cold air made it feel like the middle of winter. It was too cold for Sacajawea to carry Pompey on her back in his cradleboard. She held him next to her inside her blanket, and with her other hand, now numb with cold, she tried to guide her stumbling horse.

The captains stopped to discuss their situation. It had taken them a week to get this far up the mountain. It would take them at least four more days to reach Traveller's Rest. If they got lost, they would die, and their reports for President Jefferson might never be found. They decided they couldn't risk going any farther without a guide.

It was a sad moment when the Corps of Discovery turned to head back down the mountain. This was the first time they had ever been defeated by difficulties during the whole trip, and they were all horribly depressed.

They camped below the mountains while Drewyer rode out to find the two Nez Percé chiefs who had promised to guide them. When he returned, the captains were happy to see that a brother of Cut Nose had come, too. With their three guides, the party set out once again to try to cross the mountains.

# A GUIDE TO THE YELLOWSTONE

At the foot of the mountains, the Nez Percé set fire to some dry fir trees. The tall trees looked like a display of fireworks against the night sky. Burning the trees would bring good luck and fair weather, the Indians said.

On June 26, 1806, the Corps reached the spot where they had turned back nine days earlier. During that time, four feet of the snow had melted. The Indians hurried the crew along a ridge. They said they knew of a good spot to camp, but the expedition had to move quickly to get there by nightfall. Sure enough, the Indians led them to a place where there was a stream and grass for the horses.

To the crew's surprise, the snow made traveling toward the pass quicker. Although it was slippery, the snow was easier to walk on than the rocks and fallen trees had been. They pushed on and reached Traveller's Rest in three days. Here Lewis and Clark had decided to split the expedition into two parties.

Lewis would take a short route that Toby had showed them back to the Great Falls, then explore Maria's River. Clark planned to return to the Three Forks, going the same way the expedition had come. From there, he'd explore the Yellowstone

River. Everyone would meet again where the Yellowstone joined the Missouri River near what is now the border between Montana and North Dakota. At that point, the Corps would be about 250 miles from Fort Mandan.

By dividing into two groups, the captains could explore more of the Louisiana Territory and give President Jefferson a more complete report. But the plan was dangerous because the Corps was entering unfriendly Sioux territory. Because the two groups were smaller, they were easier for the Indians to attack. Members of the Corps would have to be on their guard every minute.

On July 3, the two parties said goodbye to their Nez Percé friends and set out on their separate journeys. Sacajawea and eighteen-month-old Pompey traveled with Captain Clark. He needed her to interpret and help steer his party through her people's land. Clark also took forty-nine of the horses.

He found a trail the Flathead Indians had told him about. It was a slightly shorter route back to the Jefferson River, where the Corps had left some supplies. After crossing what we now know as Gibbon's Pass, however, the road led through an open plain where the Indian tracks they were following went off in every direction. Clark didn't know which way to go.

Sacajawea had been to this plain many times when she was a child. Her people often came here to gather camas roots and hunt beaver, she told Clark. She showed him a creek to follow which led

81

to higher ground. There they would see a gap in the mountains. Once they passed through this gap, they'd see a high mountain covered with snow.

Clark ordered the party off in the direction in which Sacajawea pointed. The next afternoon, they made their way through the gap. As they emerged onto open ground, there before them loomed the tall, snow-capped mountain, just as she had said. It took them only one more day to reach their old camp.

Clark was delighted! Using the Flatheads' trail and Sacajawea's mountain pass, he had found the quickest, easiest route from Traveller's Rest to the Jefferson River. He knew that it was a good route for wagons and thought that settlers might even build a trading post here one day.

The men dug up the supplies they had buried here and set about repairing the canoes. As Sacajawea explored the woods, she noticed some carrot-like roots growing nearby, which she gathered for dinner. The next morning part of the group set out on the Jefferson River. The rest rode along the bank with the horses.

Sacajawea watched as they passed Beaver's Head Rock and came to the Three Forks, where Clark divided up his party. He instructed some of his men to take the canoes and continue up the Missouri River. The others, including Sacajawea, went with him by horse to find the Yellowstone River.

Clark found himself on another plain where several Indian trails criss-crossed and led to different gaps in the mountains. When Sacajawea showed him which one he should take, he didn't hesitate even though that pass was farther away. Sacajawea was his "pilot through this country."

Along the way, Clark became confused again about their direction. Sacajawea pointed out a buffalo trail they should follow. The trail led right to the pass. On the other side, they found the Yellowstone River. Now Clark knew it was just a short distance by land between the Three Forks of the Missouri and the Yellowstone. Thanks to Sacajawea he had found a good road and an easy way through the mountains.

Sacajawea's gap, known as Bozeman Pass, is near what is now Livingston, Montana. Many years after she guided Captain Clark through the pass, the Northern Pacific Railroad ran a train track through the mountains there.

Sacajawea didn't see her people on the return trip. She knew they were hidden in the mountains. The Shoshoni usually fished for salmon there during the summer, but Clark didn't make a special trip to try to find them. Would she ever have a chance to see her brother and nephew again?

They camped by the Yellowstone. In the morning they woke up to discover that Indians had slipped into camp and taken half their horses! Clark split up his group once again. Sergeant Pryor and three men rode off for Fort Mandan with the remaining horses. Clark, Sacajawea, and the rest paddled off down the Yellowstone in two dugouts they had made.

The next afternoon the boats came to a tremendous rock. It was about two hundred feet high and eight hundred feet around. Its sides went straight up, and the top of it was completely flat. It was a sacred place to the Indians, and they had carved figures of animals and special objects all over it. When Clark climbed to the top, he found they had made two ceremonial piles of stones.

For a while, Captain Clark sat on the rock, spellbound by the view. When he climbed down, he carved his name and the date, July 25, 1806, in the rock. He called it Pompey's Pillar, after the little boy he had grown so fond of. Today Pompey's Pillar is a national historic landmark, sitting between the cities of Custer and Billings, Montana.

Out on the river again, they were suddenly attacked by dense swarms of mosquitoes. The crew could hardly breathe without swallowing them. Pompey's whole face was puffed up with bites! The men couldn't even hold still long enough to aim their guns at game.

When the party reached the spot where they were supposed to meet the rest of the expedition, they couldn't stay because of the mosquitoes. They left Captain Lewis a note, telling him they had moved on farther down river.

Sergeant Pryor's party arrived at the new camp—but without the horses. Just two days after they had left Captain Clark, they woke up to find every single horse gone. Once again, the Indians had made off with them during the night.

A few days later, Captain Lewis's party pulled

into camp, yelling and waving. But everyone's joy at meeting again quickly turned to horror! Lewis was lying in the boat with a terrible gunshot wound! He passed out while Captain Clark cleaned it.

Lewis's trip had been more difficult than Clark's. When he was feeling better, he described the trouble he had with a hostile group of Sioux Indians and the terrible accident that had left him wounded. He and some of his men had explored Maria's River as planned. Coming back, they ran into eight Sioux with a herd of horses! Lewis convinced the Indians to camp with them that night. He figured that if they were all together, he and his men couldn't be ambushed in their sleep.

That night Lewis and his men took turns keeping watch. At dawn, the last guard was dozing, and Lewis himself was asleep. The Indians had been waiting for this chance and grabbed the white men's guns. In a flash the white men were awake and fighting! They stabbed one Sioux and shot another. The rest ran for the horses, but not before firing back a couple of shots. Lewis felt a bullet whiz by his ear!

After the Indians fled, the crew saddled up the best horses and galloped off. There was no time to lose! The Indians would be coming for them with a larger war party. They had to warn the rest of the Corps! Lewis and his men barely stopped to rest. They vowed that they would tie their horses together if they were attacked! They would all live or die together!

Part of the expedition was waiting for them

just past the Great Falls. Quickly they dug up the canoes and supplies they had buried earlier, hopped into the boats, and took off down the Missouri. They found Clark's notes telling them he was farther down the river, and hurried on to meet him.

They stopped long enough for Lewis and Cruzatte to go ashore to hunt. The nearsighted boatman mistook Lewis for an elk and shot him! The bullet went clear through his thigh and buttock. At first Lewis thought the Sioux had found them. Cruzatte was mortified to learn he'd shot his captain!

All during this dangerous trip Lewis had escaped injury from the rough rivers, wild animals, illness, and unfriendly Indians. Now, only a few days from the end of the expedition, he had been shot—by one of his own men!

Lewis had cleaned his wound as best he could. That night he had a fever and couldn't be moved from the boat because of the pain. By the time they caught up with Captain Clark, his leg and hip were stiff. After a night's rest, the Corps made Lewis as comfortable as possible in a boat and set out for Fort Mandan.

# GOODBYE AGAIN

On August 14, 1806, Sacajawea began to see the familiar sight of corn fields. As her boat glided past the round, earthen lodges of the Minnetaree and Mandan villages, the expedition began shouting and shooting off their guns. Indians ran to the shore and waved joyfully at the white men who were now brown from the sun and half naked in their tattered elkskin clothes.

Sacajawea was not the same person who had left Fort Mandan a year and a half earlier. She had been an obedient slave girl when she left, but she was returning a valuable member of an important expedition. As she and the crew stepped out of the boats the Indians gathered around them. Her neighbors and friends wanted to look at Pompey and hear about her adventures.

Sacajawea had made a big difference in the success of the expedition. She had translated at important Indian councils and helped the white men and the Indians understand each other's words and ways better. Without her, Lewis and Clark might not have gotten horses from Cameahwait. And they wouldn't have known that the leader planned to leave them stranded in the mountains—until it was too late.

She had guided the Corps to the Shoshoni and, later, had shown Clark the best routes through her people's territory. All along the way, she found healthful fruits and vegetables that provided necessary vitamins for the crew's diet. She had also protected the Corps from Indian attacks. She and Pompey had been a symbol of peace to many of the Indian tribes who might have thought the expedition was a war party. Just the presence of this strong, quiet woman had calmed and inspired the crew.

But it was the end of the trip for Sacajawea. The captains were ready to go meet with President Jefferson. They had maps and journals describing every mile they had traveled and all the people they had met. They offered to give Sacajawea and Charbonneau a ride to St. Louis, but Charbonneau said he had no way of making a living there.

Captain Clark wanted to take Pompey with him. He had become so attached to Sacajawea's "beautiful, promising child" that he couldn't bear to part with the little boy. He offered to raise Pompey and give him an education. But Pompey was only a year and a half old and still nursing. In another year, when he was weaned, Sacajawea said she would bring him to Clark.

Charbonneau was paid five hundred dollars and thirty-three cents, good wages for the time. Sacajawea was paid nothing for her services since, as far as the government was concerned, she was simply Charbonneau's wife.

On August 17, Sacajawea waved goodbye to the Corps of Discovery boats as they took off for St. Louis. It was the last leg of their astounding adven-

89

ture. Before Lewis and Clark, no white men had ever crossed that part of the country. The Lewis and Clark expedition had done it twice. They had traveled down the wide Missouri and the raging Columbia rivers. They had found a way to get around the Great Falls, the Celilo Falls, and the Cascades. They had lodged with many Indians and learned how the different tribes lived. And they had brought back specimens of plants and animals that white Americans had never seen.

The Corps of Discovery had succeeded in its goal. They had found a way to travel across the whole country by river and land. No obstacle that this wild and uncharted terrain had put in their path had stopped them. And during the whole difficult journey, Sacajawea had managed to carry and care for a baby.

The Lewis and Clark expedition became famous and so did some of the crew. But what happened to Sacajawea afterwards is mostly unrecorded.

The Red Headed Chief kept his promise to raise and educate her son, Jean Baptiste, which was Pompey's real name. Sacajawea's son grew up to be a well-educated gentleman. When Jean Baptiste was eighteen, he became friends with a German prince who was visiting America and traveled with him in Europe for six years.

When he returned to the United States, he became a fur dealer and a guide. For a while, Jean Baptiste lived in California and became mayor of Mission San Luis Rey. In 1866, when he was sixty-one years old, he headed for Oregon to look for gold, but he became sick and died that same year.

Sacajawea's husband, Toussaint Charbonneau, continued to be an interpreter and fur trader. He was last heard of in 1839, when he was about eighty years old. That year he turned up at the Indian affairs offices in St. Louis and asked the superintendent there for his back pay as an interpreter for the Mandans.

But what about Sacajawea?

Most experts now agree that on April 2, 1811, Sacajawea set out with Charbonneau on a Missouri river expedition. She later settled at a fur trade post that was not far from where she had joined the Lewis and Clark expedition nearly seven years earlier. These experts believe that Sacajawea died there on December 20, 1812, of a "putrid fever."

Some stories say Sacajawea returned to her people and lived to be nearly 100 years old. We will never know, for certain, if these stories are true.

What we do know for certain is that the country Sacajawea helped to explore did not forget her. Today, there are at least three mountains, two lakes, and twenty-three monuments named for her. Sacajawea will live on forever in America's history.

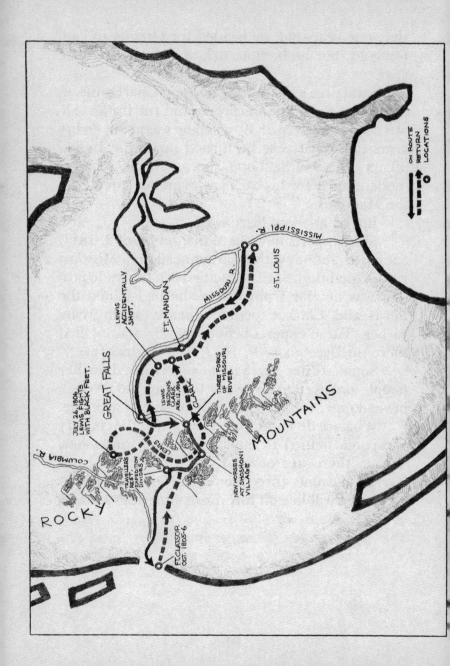

MISSISSIPPI R.

MISSOURI R.

ST. LOUIS

FT. MANDAN

LEWIS
ACCIDENTALLY
SHOT.

JULY 26, 1806
LEWIS FIGHTS
WITH BLACK FEET.

GREAT FALLS

LEWIS REJOINS
CLARK ON
AUG. 12, 1806

CLARK

TRAVELERS
REST

EXPEDITION
DIVIDES

THREE FORKS
OF MISSOURI
RIVER

LEWIS

COLUMBIA R.

NEW HORSES
AT SHOSHONI
VILLAGE

ROCKY

MOUNTAINS

FT. CLATSOP
OCT. 1805-6

ON ROUTE
RETURN
LOCATIONS